Refuel, Recharge, and Re-energize:

*Your Guide to
Taking Back Control of
Your Time and Energy*

❋

Erin Owen, MBA

*Teri,
Here's to your
positive transformation!*

Produced in the United States of America

Owen, Erin
Refuel, Recharge, and Re-energize:
Your Guide to
Taking Back Control of
Your Time and Energy / Erin Owen, MBA

ISBN 978-0-9863581-8-0

To order books,
email Connect@ErinOwen.com
or visit www.ErinOwen.com

In Gratitude…

*To all the wonderful people in my life who helped
make this book a reality.*

I dedicate this book…

*To all the teachers (living and passed on) who have transmitted to
me the wisdom of the ancient Eastern philosophies and practices that
inspire my work in the world.*

Thank you all!

Contents

Preface to the Second Edition 7

Introduction 9

Chapter One
Reboot Your Internal Computer Daily 11

Chapter Two
Feed Your Body to Boost Brain Power and Fuel Business Success . . . 16

Chapter Three
Own Your Calendar So It Doesn't Own You 21

Chapter Four
De-clutter to De-stress and Fuel Creativity for Your Success 25

Chapter Five
Breathe! 29

Chapter Six
Cultivate More Yin to Balance the Yang 32

Chapter Seven
Mindfully Monitor What Matters 35

Conclusion 42

Take it to the Next Level 44

Preface to the Second Edition

If you are desiring more ease and freedom in your life, then this book is for you.

Feeling exhausted and overwhelmed most days of your life is not a sustainable way of living. You know this already, but you may not know what to do about it. All you need is 5 minutes a day (see Chapter 1) to regain control of your time and energy.

We all seem to be suffering from *presenteeism**—the condition of being in the room at work (or at home) but not really being there. Your mind is distracted by all you have to do. Your smart phone, tablet, and computer unceasingly demand your attention. You can't focus long enough to finish a thought or sentence, let alone complete a project. And forget about connecting in a meaningful way with the most important people in your life.

If you are in a leadership role in your organization, your family, your community, the ripple effect and total impact of your overwhelm can be exponential. When you are not sleeping well, when your brain is sluggish, when your mood is subdued or sour, you perform at a sub-optimal level in all the roles you play in your life. Your general state of "overwhelm" unintentionally and negatively affects everyone around you and the performance of your organization.

Most of us think about sustainability as an issue related only to the environment. But the truth is when you begin to make more mindful choices for yourself, you become more aware of the interconnectedness of all things. You begin working and living in a more sustainable way. You make smarter choices about the food you eat, the products you buy, the markets you enter (if you are in business). You start to tune into the impact of all your choices on other human beings and on the planet.

The first edition of this book was dedicated to "conscious entrepre-neurs", but I have heard over and over again—from readers, from clients, from members of the audience where I am invited to speak—that the key ideas in this book are relevant to anyone who is strug-gling with feeling overwhelmed and disconnected.

I hope you find great satisfaction in experimenting with the simple tips I share in this concise book. You may even surprise yourself and finish reading it! (When was the last time you finished a book?)

If you prefer to listen to an audio-recorded version of each chapter and dive-in further, be sure and check out the complementary au-dio and video resources at ErinOwen.com/BookResources. The final section titled "Take it to the Next Level" also details how you can access additional resources, strategies, and support for refueling, re-charging, and re-energizing.

I look forward to hearing how the ideas and practices in this book help you shift from a dark place of overwhelm to a lighter state of ease and freedom, more in control of your time and energy.

Erin
May 2015

*"Presenteeism" is a term coined by Paul Hemp, the author of a 2004 article titled "Presenteism: At Work – But Out of it", published in the *Harvard Business Review*. In the article, Helm states that presenteeism "costs U.S. companies over $150 billion a year--much more than absenteeism does." Learn more at hbr.org

Erin Elizabeth Owen

Introduction

These days, life is full.

New technology makes our lives easier and allows us to be more productive. However, it also makes it more difficult for us to discern the boundaries between work-life, home-life and everything in between. As a result, our schedules are jam-packed, giving us little room to breathe.

This is especially true for leaders. When you are responsible for the bottom line, the demands and expectations of life can seem overwhelming. And, if you also have a family to manage, the complexity is even greater.

Some days it can feel like everything is running so smoothly and then…BOOM! It all falls apart.

This intensity—this pace that we're living at in the modern world—is driving us to the edge. It's up to you to decide if you want to continue feeling overwhelmed by life or, instead, take a journey with me to explore how you can live and work in a new, better way. A way that enables you to achieve your highest potential and make your positive mark on the world, all while regaining control of your time and energy.

In this book, I share how the Eastern concept of Yin and Yang applies to how we live and work in the Western world. I reveal performance secrets inspired by Eastern practices across a number of countries and thousands of years of history. At the root of these practices are mindfulness (being present), breathing and balance. All the practices are simple, approachable, flexible, portable and, best of all, free.

After reading this short book and experimenting with the practices that appeal most to you, you will experience a sense of ease, control and peace that allows you to be much more productive in your business and, ideally, a more pleasant person all around. Ultimately, you'll be closer to performing at your optimum level and living your life in an enjoyable, meaningful, sustainable way.

Thank you for believing in yourself to make this small investment of time and energy. Why do I thank you? We are all connected, so I know that when you succeed, we all succeed.

Namaste,

Erin

Chapter One
Reboot Your Internal Computer Daily

❋

Space. Your [first and] last frontier.

In this first chapter, we focus on your inner space, that is, your mind. It is a frontier worth exploring on a daily basis.

Typically, the mind actively thinks about such things as the to-do list, a conversation you had yesterday, a conversation you need to have tomorrow, fears, memories, hopes, etc. But how often do you purposefully sit quietly and clear your mind? What I'm talking about here is rebooting your internal computer—your brain—on a daily basis by cultivating a quiet space for your mind. When you do this, you give yourself an opportunity to refuel, recharge and re-energize.

To create this quiet space in your mind, you must create space in your schedule (more on this topic in chapter three) Why exactly is it important to do this? And how do you make the time when there is so much to do?

The Why

You wake up in the middle of the night with a racing mind and a feeling of anxiety about things you forgot to do or things you need to do the following day. It's nearly impossible to go back to sleep once your brain starts plowing through your to-do list.

Once awake, you feel the only way to get everything done is to multitask. In the evening, it might be common for you to be simultaneously tossing something together for dinner (if you even have time to do that), checking email, overseeing (sort of) what the kids are doing and checking in with your partner about schedules. Whew! It's exhausting just to think about living this way on a regular basis.

If you want to enjoy life more, be more effective in your work and get more done, then, ironically, it is essential that you do *less*, by setting aside some time and entering that amazing, mystical space commonly known as your mind.

I know. It seems like I'm asking for the unattainable. How can you possibly do one more thing? It might feel that way now, but trust me. There is a sweet kind of magic that unfolds when you cultivate space for your mind and reboot your internal computer. With regular practice, time seems to slow down and stretch beyond the comprehension of the left brain, allowing you to be more present and on top of your game.

Scientists have proven numerous times that the brain performs better when it has time to rest quietly and focus on just one thing. The ancient practices of meditation and yoga are among many that recognize the importance of turning inward to enhance performance.

We live in a society that considers multitasking to be an effective method for getting more done. However, the reality is that you are less likely to remember the key details of a conversation if you are simultaneously checking messages on a handheld device. You are more likely to miss your desired destination if you are reading a text on your phone while walking down the street. And your odds of getting into a traffic accident are significantly increased if you are talking on the phone while riding a bike or driving a car. So, is doing more really helping you get more done?

When you take time out for yourself on a daily basis to refuel, recharge and re-energize, you create a more enjoyable, meaningful and productive life. This is possible when you learn my simple strategies for taking back control of your time and your energy.

So let's look at how to do this in a simple, enjoyable and sustainable way that fits your lifestyle and boosts your performance to a more optimum level.

The How

First, you need to pick a time of day when you are least likely to get derailed by distractions. For many, the best time is early in the morning. Initially, it might seem impossible to carve out an extra 5-10 minutes before you dive into your day. However, in a short period of time you'll begin to notice the cumulative benefits of your practice, and you'll find it becomes easier to carve out the space you need to reboot.

You can experiment with each of the following methods, even combining a few or all of them. Feel free to choose the practice that best serves you in the moment.

✳ Sit and breathe. Find a relatively peaceful spot in your home to sit quietly. Just sit and focus on your breath. If you prefer, you can formally practice any type of meditation; however, just focusing on the breath can be a powerful and positively transformative experience.

Set a timer or simply check a watch or the clock. Focus on the breath as it moves in through the nose and trace its path as it moves through and then releases from your body. Allow each breath to be a bit longer, a bit more expansive in the body. Imagine that each inhalation draws in the exact nourishment you need, while each exhalation carries away whatever is no longer serving you.

If your mind easily wanders to this or that thought, then know this— you are perfectly normal. You can train your mind to focus on the breath by quietly saying to yourself "inhale" as you breathe in and "exhale" as you breathe out. Or pick another set of words or phrases to pair with each part of the breath, such as "here" (inhale) and "now" (exhale), or "thank" (inhale) and "you" (exhale), or "everything is" (inhale) "complete" (exhale) ... you get the idea.

I've recorded several short audio meditations to support you in exploring your internal terrain. Visit ErinOwen.com/BookResources to listen in or download to a mobile device.

✳ Write in a journal or notebook. Sit comfortably—prop yourself on pillows right there in bed or nestle into your favorite soft chair. Give yourself a few minutes to write anything that comes to mind, without editing or judging or expecting. Ideally, avoid using a computer for this exercise and just write. By doing so, you'll unload the contents of your mind, acknowledging in a subtle way that its contributions are important enough to capture on paper, yet, at the same time, creating space for your brain to breathe.

Next, spend a few minutes writing about something positive that warms you up inside, excites you or inspires your creative energy. You might make a list of all that you are grateful for in your life. Or, you can write about your hopes and dreams with as little or as much detail as makes you feel good in the moment. Alternatively, perhaps you find yourself spontaneously writing a piece of content relevant to your home or work life. Just let it flow. Do this without editing, without judgment and without any expectations.

✳ Walk outside. Especially in the early morning hours, when the earth is turning to reveal the sun coming up over the horizon, there is a beautiful quiet that inspires the cultivation of space, relaxation and openness in your inner world. Dress appropriately for the weather and give yourself permission to wander without a fixed destination. Enjoy the simple miracle of breathing and moving your body and give yourself over to tuning in to the sounds of nature (or the waking city), observing the changing shapes, textures and colors of your surroundings.

Engaging in one or more of these practices on a regular basis, or ezperimenting with other similar practices that inspire you, will help you create a nice rhythm of certainty with your inner space-diving rituals. You will discover that the unique personal benefits waiting for you become more evident and multiply over time.

The Bottom Line

Take back control of your time and energy. Slow down, quiet your mind, and enjoy greater productivity and a more enjoyable way of living.

Further Resources

Download or listen to an audio version of Chapter One at ErinOwen. com/BookResources. Access a selection of short, guided meditations that are guaranteed to leave you feeling calm, centered, grounded and ready to take on any challenge that comes your way. And look at the final few pages of this book to learn how to take it to the next level.

Chapter Two

Feed Your Body to Boost
Brain Power and Fuel Business Success

✳

*Starting your day with a warm breakfast not only
sparks your digestive fire, but also boosts your metabolism,
brain function and immunity—all critical for
supercharging you—the engine behind your business,
your passion, your purpose.*

You've known this since grade school—breakfast is the most important meal of the day. Yet, do you treat your first meal of the day like it's optional?

Cultivating a grounding ritual around the beverages and whole foods that create the foundation for each day's performance is the focus of this second chapter. Whether this is something you resist or commit to, experimenting with different breakfast foods will help you catapult your daily potential from "just getting by" to "hitting the ball out of the park" time and again.

The Why

That anxiety-invoking laundry list of to-do items that hits you like a speeding truck in the wee hours might launch you into skipping breakfast and diving directly into your most urgent responsibility, armed with only a cup of coffee.

That rush of caffeine that wakes up your brain and spurs you into action also shuts down digestion. When your digestive process stops, you get a false sensation that you are sated and can go without food at least until lunch. In addition, your metabolism, fearing that you might be in a state of starvation, signals your body to hold onto any excess energy, which is usually in the form of fat.

Skipping breakfast might save you time and money in the short-run. Unfortunately, skipping breakfast forces your body to draw upon precious and finite life essence to sustain you. That is, until you hit the wall—exhausted and hungry. Then, you reach for whatever calories are nearby, usually high-sugar and high-fat snack foods, and consume them to survive the day.

You repeat this general pattern for days, weeks, months or even years. You may even pride yourself on the limits to which you can push yourself to finish the next deadline, project or critical proposal that you are certain will launch you from "ho-hum-dum" to stardom.

But at some point, you break down and get sick. Over time, the repeated pattern of pushing-pushing-pushing and crashing escalates such that the length of time between colds and trips to the pharmacy decreases, and the severity of each bout worsens. You end up depending on medications, over-the-counter and prescription. You consider this to be normal because everyone around you does the same thing. You can't imagine any other way to do your work.

If this describes you, I feel for you because I was once living that way, too. If you are like I was back then, your inner drive is so relentless that even if you have a sense that this can't go on much longer, you simply don't know where to begin or how to turn things around.

The harsh reality is that this way of living and working is not sustainable. Your body will break down to the point where, depending on your constitution and genetic pre-disposition, you end up overweight, hypertensive and/or sugar-sensitive. Furthermore, you might contract any of a long list of undesirable chronic or potentially life-threatening diseases, such as diabetes, cancer or heart disease.

You don't want that. You certainly would not consciously choose that fate. Yet, by getting caught up in the daily spin of frenetic activity and skipping breakfast, you are unwittingly choosing to undermine your immediate and long-term performance, thereby dimming your inner light and diminishing the potential impact you could have on the world.

If you want to repair and revive the engine behind your business, your passion, your purpose, you must start each day with a warm breakfast. Doing so will not only spark your digestive fire, it will also boost your metabolism, fuel your brainpower and support a healthy, well-functioning immune system.

Let's look at how you can do this—and adopt some other simple, straightforward practices—in a way that works for you and your lifestyle.

The How

Start gradually by experimenting with different breakfast foods— even those that might seem outside the norm. Take note of how eating a warm breakfast in general affects you, and how specific foods affect your energy level throughout the entire day, not just the morning hours. Allow yourself at least five minutes to sit down and focus solely on eating, and reap the rewards as you quickly refuel, recharge and re-energize from the inside out.

※ What to Eat in the Morning. Contrary to the common grab-and-go practice, skip the carbs and start your first meal of the day with a whole food source of protein. For almost everyone, a high-protein breakfast will sustain your energy throughout the full day and reduce (or even eliminate) sugar cravings.

Great sources of breakfast protein include eggs, beans and legumes of all kinds and even certain whole grains that also contain all of the essential amino acids your body needs to make protein—quinoa, amaranth and buckwheat. My favorite make-ahead recipes that require little prep time in the morning can be found at ErinOwen.com/BookResources.

Why a Warm Breakfast? I recommend your breakfast be warm because warm foods are energetically grounding and stabilizing, and eating in this way will kick-start your day in a solid, steady way. Also, your belly wants to be a 100° pot of warm soup. If the food isn't warm when it goes in, your body has to expend extra resources to raise the temperature before healthy digestion can begin. So, conserve your energy and boost your performance by beginning each morning in this great way.

❈ What to Drink in the Morning. I may not be able to convince you to quit your coffee habit, but I encourage you to wait on that first sip of caffeine until about an hour after you finish eating. Really!

If you're open to the idea of cutting back on or eventually eliminating coffee, consider this: research has linked excess caffeine intake to cardiovascular problems, adrenal exhaustion, emotional issues, blood sugar imbalance, gastrointestinal concerns, nutritional deficiencies, and more. It even exacerbates the negative effects of stress. I wish it weren't so.

Instead, clear out the junk that builds up overnight (and over the *years* of less-than-ideal grab-n-go dining), by beginning each morning with one or more of the following *before* you sit down and eat:

- Eight to sixteen ounces of warm or hot water mixed with the juice of one fresh lemon

- Eight to sixteen ounces of ginger tea, made either with 1-2 bags of the store-bought, dried herbal variety or by simmering freshly sliced ginger (to taste) in the water on the stovetop for 10 minutes, then straining.

✳ How to Nourish Yourself in the Morning. Sit down once a week (once a month after you've developed a consistent breakfast habit) to plan what you'll eat each morning of the week.

Shop for any ingredients you don't already have in the pantry and, ideally, stock up on dried or canned beans, whole grains (which can keep for up to six months in a dry, cool, dark storage place) and any dried herbs and spices you enjoy adding for that morning *zing*.

Cook more than you need for that week and freeze half for another week (be sure to label and date your extra portions in a freezer-size, air-tight container) and put the rest in the refrigerator to warm up on the stovetop for each morning's sustenance.

Plan for at least five minutes (but ideally 10 to 15) to sit quietly, with feet on the floor and a tall spine. Take three deep, slow breaths to center yourself and focus solely on chewing and enjoying your food. Set aside electronic devices and give yourself permission to fully receive the nutrients from your food. Savor the flavors and appreciate yourself for taking the time to create a performance-boosting foundation for your day.

The Bottom Line

Catapult yourself above and beyond your "barely getting by" way of living by starting each day with a warm, nourishing breakfast to feed your body, boost your brain power and fuel the success of your business.

Further Resources

Download or listen to an audio version of chapter two and access my favorite, time-saving, performance-boosting breakfast recipes at ErinOwen.com/BookResources. Learn how else you can take action at the end of this book.

Chapter Three
Own Your Calendar So It Doesn't Own You

❋

Conserve and build your vital pool of life force energy (prana/qi) by focusing your attention and taking the path of least resistance.

In this chapter, you'll learn how to conserve and grow your vital stock pile of life force energy by changing how you manage your time.

This secret sauce, called *prana* in the yoga tradition and *qi* (pronounced "chee") in the Chinese medicine and Daoist traditions/practices, is what quietly and powerfully enables you to breathe and function normally on a daily basis. It can also *dramatically* transform what's possible for you and your passions in this lifetime.

Using simple time management strategies is a straightforward way to not only nurture your life force energy but also realize that time is neither linear nor finite. By slowly and enjoyably changing the way you manage your time, you can positively shift to a higher level of functioning and productivity.

It all begins with your calendar.

The Why

The words "I wish I could, but I don't have time" commonly, and regrettably, have taken the place of the instinctive and spontaneous "yes, let's do it" of the much younger you.

The weight of the shoulds and can'ts make breathing difficult sometimes, and often, sadly, it pulls you away from the inner spark that originally put you on your path or drove you to start the business of your dreams.

The list of things you wish you could do for yourself, with friends and family, or even for your home, grows longer each day, and you find yourself making vague promises about the timing and circumstances under which you'll finally start that exercise class, go on that trip or tackle that bathroom remodeling project.

Figuring out how to make every minute count may be a constant source of stress for you. But, there's hope. Taking a different tack on time management is an incredibly useful and potentially life-changing skill that can quickly yield positive, tangible results.

So, set aside your current ideas and beliefs about how time works and what is possible, and I will share with you three proven strategies that can refuel, recharge and re-energize your prana/qi tank.

The How

✳ Put yourself in your calendar first. That's right. Make what you know is central for your self-care the anchors of your dynamic, changing life. Your list of self-care activities might include a form of exercise or centering activity such as yoga, prayer or meditation. Or, perhaps you block out time with your partner, best friend or children. Whatever it is, map out scheduled and carefully guarded appointments in your calendar for these daily or weekly commitments to yourself.

After these anchors are firmly in place, then begin to build in focused time blocks for your work. This is critical: carefully guard your precious qi-boosting activities.

For more guidance on how to do this and tips on getting support from your clients, customers and family members, visit ErinOwen. com/BookResources.

✳ Do one thing at a time. This is the antithesis of multitasking and goes against every technological development in our modern way of living and working. However, doing one thing at a time (single-tasking) will ensure that you are ultimately much more productive, effective and successful in your endeavors. I guarantee that you will feel less scattered, more centered and calm, more joyful and re-connected with your purpose and your passions.

How to do this? Take baby steps at first. Build as you go. Schedule just two or three blocks of time every day for when you will read and respond to email. Consistently demarcate and communicate when you will meet with clients and customers. Set aside set days or times of day to focus on networking and business-building activities. Make appointments with yourself for focused activities with concrete parameters, such as writing content for one hour, three times a week; painting or creating another form of artwork for five hours, two times a week; or engaging in creative brainstorming and design work for 30 to 45 minutes daily. Dedicate regular blocks of time in your schedule for the "secret sauce" of your work.

✳ Keep one calendar and update it daily. If reading this makes you laugh or take a deep sigh, then know that I'm especially talking to you! It's time to stop straddling the paper-digital divide and choose which side of the chasm you will stand on. Choose wisely and make sure it energizes you and supports the way in which your clients and colleagues work with you. Or, if you are carrying around multiple devices, such as phones, tablets and laptops, consolidate! Stop making excuses, find someone to help you and do it today. Yes, today.

The Bottom Line

You *are* the heart of the work you do, and how you manage your time ultimately drains you or revitalizes you. Experiment with at least one new approach.

Further Resources

Find additional resources and an audio version of chapter three at ErinOwen.com/BookResources. And learn how you can build on these ideas in the final pages of this book.

Chapter Four
De-clutter to De-stress and Fuel Creativity for Your Success

✻

Make room for more free flow of creative ideas and inspiration for your business by getting rid of that which no longer serves you.

Whether you look at it from an Eastern energetic point of view or a more mainstream one, the reality is the same:

All that clutter in your physical and digital space clogs your creative pipes, and that carries with it a price. It negatively affects your mental health and prevents you from following through on the next big idea.

Finding easy, manageable ways to establish and maintain order in your home and work environment will reduce your stress, make your physical space more inviting to guests and clients, and generate room for unlimited amounts of creative ideas and energy.

The Why

Your focus is on what's next—getting to the next meeting, responding to an important email or new client order, returning a phone call, arriving at your child's school on time for pick-up. You rarely—if ever—have time to finish a sentence or thought, let alone follow each task through to its completion. It often feels as if you are two steps behind and running late.

As a result, everything is in a state of disarray: your desk, your car, your bedroom, your kitchen counters, your workbag, and even your email and electronic folders. The piles are growing and unwieldy, and your spillover and chaotic life are driving your loved ones and workmates crazy.

You can't find key documents, you misplace critical business cards, your work clothes are wrinkled in a pile on the floor, and you're wasting time and energy dealing with the aftermath of Tsunami You!

Where in this picture is there mental and physical space to tap into the next big idea for your work, the words for the perfect subject line to get your next client to actually open your email, or the energy to be able to think on your feet in critical conversations? Nowhere!

You wonder, where do I begin? And how do I avoid drowning in clutter before becoming a candidate for the next episode of a reality TV show about hoarders?

Read on to discover some of the key principles I share with my private clients to tame the clutter, break free of the stress and exhaustion clutter causes and reclaim access to a never-ending flow of creative inspiration for your business.

The How

✳ "Own Place": Make a dedicated place for:

- Documents that require action (e.g., bills to be paid),

- Important papers (e.g., incorporation documentation and taxes from the past seven years)

- Active work for a current client or customer

Erin Elizabeth Owen

- Items related to an important system for your business (e.g., tracking leads)

For all the rest, either put it in storage (e.g., old tax documents or past client/customer materials), or—much better—get rid of it (e.g., articles that you will honestly never read again, hard copies of what you can access online, etc.).

The things you keep should be clearly and appropriately named in an appropriate "place," such as an electronic folder, physical binder or file folder.

※ "One Touch": For each email, piece of physical mail, fax or voicemail, only "touch" it once and take immediate action to put it in its "place." The action you take when you touch it just once will be one of the following: file it away, recycle it, shred it, donate it, hand it down or toss it. For actions that require your immediate attention, take action only when you know you have a few moments to either reply or create a reminder on your calendar to follow-up or truly be present for the conversation. For example, listen to the voicemail or read the email only when you can respond. Only open the bill when you are ready to put it in the "bills to be paid" folder—better yet, pay it on the spot!

※ Make it a habit. Respecting the "Own Place" and "One Touch" principles will prevent you from unnecessarily coming back to the same email/voicemail/bill/etc again and again, thereby further conserving your energy so that it can be channeled into more lucrative and enjoyable uses of your time and mental focus.

Dedicate just a few minutes each day to put things in their place or get rid of them. View this as a critical practice that shores up the creativity pillar of your work.

Just imagine how light and energized you will feel once these practices are in place, creating a sense of freedom and hope that will fuel your creativity.

The Bottom Line

Declutter your physical and digital environments to free up creative energy and inspire new possibilities in your life and in your business.

Further Resources

For the full list of Personal Organization principles I share with my private clients, as well as the audio version of chapter four, visit ErinOwen.com/BookResources. And flip to the end of this book to learn how to receive additional free resources.

Chapter Five
Breathe!

*It is said that in a single 1-hour yoga practice,
you breathe in more oxygen than the average
person breathes in during a whole day.*

You need to breathe. That much is obvious.

But did you know that breathing is the primary way in which life force energy (*prana/qi*) is carried into and throughout the body?

So breathing is not only about driving oxygen to every cell in the body, but is essential for boosting your life force, revitalizing and activating your highest potential.

The Why

Exactly how the breath and qi work together is still a bit of a mystery for most of us, but we know that you must breathe deeply and fully to think clearly, to be physically active, for your organs to function properly and for you to have a deep pool of energy to make your mark on the world.

And yet breathing is usually an afterthought—all the distractions and stresses of your complex life result in you using just one-third of your breath capacity. We tend to hold the breath or breathe shallowly when we are feeling angry, stressed or upset, resulting in less oxygen getting into our bodies.

Less oxygen in your system creates more tension in your muscles, stiffer joints, feelings of "spaciness" and un-groundedness, making you grumpier, less focused, and less effective. Not to mention that your shallow breathing also contributes to increased frequency of sickness and rigid thinking.

When you hold your breath or fail to breathe in fully, you keep your emotions at bay, thereby cutting off an incredibly important resource of information that you need to make smart decisions.

Luckily, breath is readily accessible, free of cost, and portable—so trying the breathing exercises I share in this chapter is an easy way to almost instantly refuel, recharge and re-energize yourself—anywhere, anytime.

The How

✳ Actively move your body for 18-22 minutes at least three times a week (if not daily). This gets your blood flowing and clears away fog and fatigue. Instead of hunting down another caffeine injection, try taking a brisk walk as a mid-day break—ideally around 2 or 3 p.m., or whenever your energy level is naturally low.

✳ Lay on your back with your legs leaning against a wall, rest your hands on your belly and focus all of your awareness on your breath—expanding your belly up and out like a balloon and relaxing and releasing it as you breathe out. Stay in this position with legs up the wall and practice breathing for 3, 5 or even 10 minutes at a time.

✳ Count your breaths: Wherever you are—at your desk, on a plane, in a car, lying in bed—focus your attention on counting the length of your breaths. As you inhale, count in your mind upward from one...the less perspective you have on what's important for you and your work in the world. As you exhale, quietly count backward, matching the length of the exhalation to the length of the inhalation.

As a result, you get swept away by passing fads and what others are doing that have no real bearing on what's truly important to you.

You wake up one day and wonder how you got off track. You struggle to reclaim or rekindle that passion and inner drive that set you off on this course of life in the first place.

The Bottom Line

Breathe more often and more deeply to perform closer to your optimum level.

Further Resources

To view a video of how to do these breathing exercises, and to listen to the audio version of chapter five, visit ErinOwen.com/BookResources.

Chapter Six

Cultivate More Yin to Balance the Yang

✻

The single most YIN element in our world is water. The single most YANG side effect of our modern way of living is stress. What simple practice could you implement to be more in balance and control of your life?

Regardless of how much you know about the deeper philosophical and energetic roots of Yin and Yang, chances are you are familiar with the black and white graphic that looks like two polka-dotted sperms chasing each other in a circle!

Gaining a simple understanding of how this ancient Eastern framework applies to your life can help you let go of the old "go-go-go" way of living and working that generates diminishing results.

The Why

The more tightly scheduled your days, the more tension you feel in your body. The more constriction in your body, the less awareness you have of your body's needs for the most basic sustenance—oxygen, water, rest, sunlight and whole foods from nature—and the more disconnected you feel from the natural cycles and rhythms of life. The more disconnected you are from your body and nature, the more you stay in the heady and addictive world of thinking, with your active mind spinning in every direction. The more focused you are on the minutiae of the tasks on your "to do" list, the less perspective you have on what's important for you and your business.

As a result, you get swept away by passing fads and what others are doing (that has no real bearing on what's truly important to you).

You wake up one day and wonder how you got so off track and struggle to reclaim or rekindle that passion and inner drive that set you off on this course of running your own practice or business in the first place.

If you find yourself feeling out of balance and lost—for a moment here and there or as a more permanent condition of a longer-term imbalance—you will truly benefit from the innate brilliance of the Yin Yang philosophy through some of the simple, sustainable practices I teach my clients. These practices will help you get back into balance and release the stress and scattered thoughts that distract you from your purpose, so you can reconnect with your passion. To paraphrase Gandhi, create the change you want to see in your world.

The How

✳ If you are really inflexible in your body—either due to engaging in such strength-building, muscle-bound physical activities as weight-lifting, cycling or running or due to a lack of physical activity, then I recommend you practice yin yoga to bring your body back into balance. By settling into passive postures while sitting or lying down, the practice of *yin yoga*—for as little as 5 to 20 minutes two or three times a week—can increase flexibility, reduce stress, quiet anxiety and bring you a greater sense of balance and well-being.

To experience a few relaxing and rejuvenating yin yoga poses and access additional resources, watch the short video at ErinOwen.com/BookResources.

✳️ If your diet is made up primarily of raw food or refined sugar products (both of which, in excess, can contribute to that spacey, ungrounded feeling that makes it difficult to focus and be productive in your business), then try preparing more warm, cooked whole foods at home on the stovetop or in the oven.

✳️ If your stress level feels unmanageable, then invite in the opposite feeling through one of any number of more "yin" activities such as: a gentle massage; playing with puppies, kittens or young children; watching a silly program or movie; taking a warm bath; walking outside where you can hear nature and see green; calling a good friend; or finding another way to be more intimate with a loved one.

✳️ Drink more water. As mentioned earlier in this chapter, water is the most YIN element on the planet. If you're not sure how much water to drink, slowly work your way up from what you are currently drinking to a maximum amount of approximately your body weight divided by two (e.g., 160 lb / 2 = 80 oz of water). Notice how increasing your water intake softens the tissues of your body, improves your mind, regulates such important bodily functions as bowel movements, hydrates your dry skin and boosts your overall mental and physical energy.

The Bottom Line

Cultivate more YIN in your life to balance the YANG and take back control of your time and energy so you can live life with joy and make a difference.

Further Resources

Visit ErinOwen.com/BookResources to see a simple exercise that brings the Yin Yang framework to life so you can use it to balance yourself at any moment of the day. You'll also find a demo of some yin yoga poses and the audio recording of chapter six.

Chapter Seven
Mindfully Monitor What Matters

✳

Wherever you direct your attention, energy follows.

As you become aware of and actively track the simple practices and ways of being that support you in feeling your best and performing at your optimum, you create a toolkit that will serve you for the rest of your life.

The Why

Life feels like a rollercoaster. Sometimes the down times last only a day or two, but sometimes you feel like you're dragging around for months, or even years.

Then, one day you realize, "Hey, it doesn't have to be this way. I don't have to feel this way." You remember that before you got sucked down into that black hole, you were taking much better care of yourself and being more consistent in doing what you know works best for you.

So, why keep getting on this rollercoaster, when you could choose a smooth, cruise down the fast lane?

The How

Mindfully monitor what matters most to you and write it down.

Make a list. Your list might include writing down what you are grateful for (e.g., business revenue, new clients, weight loss, etc.) or your best self-care and energy management strategies (e.g., sleeping nine hours a night, starting each day with journaling, eating greens two times a day or exercising daily). Write it down. Make a list. And that list will become the foundation of what I call your Personal Performance PLATINUM Practices.

Building on and evolving this list of practices is a mindfulness practice in and of itself. You can look at it daily, keep copies of it in numerous places or even carry it with you on your smart phone. Reference your list when you get off track. This will bring you closer to being a Master of your highest potential.

The Bottom Line

By really working your list of Personal Performance Platinum Practices™, you will:

- Avoid getting derailed by what others are doing - what they are doing is what works for them, not you!

- Manifest more of what you want more of in your life and business

- Experience fewer and fewer setbacks

- Reduce the frequency with which you get thrown off track

- Get smarter about how to learn from these setbacks

- Recover more quickly so that from an outsider's perspective, it seems like you never lose balance

- Stay on track toward realizing the vision you have for your life and the positive impact you want your work to have on the world

Erin Elizabeth Owen

Further Resources

To learn how unique your own list of platinum practices can be, scan through the three distinct examples below.

To view my own ever-evolving personal list of Platinum Practices™ and access additional resources, visit ErinOwen.com/BookResources.

Irma's List of Platinum Practices™

Irma calls her platinum practices "Secret Weapons of Mass Expansion":

- Say "NO" to activities that don't support me

- Lower my expectations without deluding my vision - commit to my vision - and detach from the "HOW's"

- Meditation - Trusting

- Don't schedule commitments during my low energy period

- Single task

- Stop and breathe to approach each activity with a better energy

- Daily Movement

- Neat Room

- Remember: where my thoughts go my energy will follow

Domenic's List of Platinum Practices™

Notice how Domenic uses sub-categories for his different practices.

Morning ritual

- wake up at 6am

- pray

- be grateful for what I have and am going to have

- visualize happiness, peace, and abundance; feel as if I already have it

- meditate

- work out

- read

Throughout the day

- drink water

- eat healthy

- teach children something new everyday

- give more than what I receive

- take a break during the day

- thank people for all they do

- tell family I love them

- stay true to my vision

- be creative

- learn what I need to know about my business and what I love

- do from the heart

- make people smile

- listen to others

- one touch (do things one time)

- single tasking

- do what I say

- stop worrying

- be enthusiastic about everything

- talk to be listened to; use tone of voice

- make each day a successful one

Nighttime ritual

- pray

- be grateful for what I have and am going to have

- visualize happiness, peace, and abundance; feel as if I already have it

- meditate

- read

For children

- teach them who I am and what I love

- teach them Italian

- love them in the way they need to be loved

- read to them, play

- mindful eating/mindful everything

- have them experience new things

- learn arts: martial arts, meditation, yoga, music, theater

- do things with them that are meaningful, such as helping others, giving to others

- teach about God

- meditate with them

- make each day a successful one

For my wife

- be in the relationship more

- make her laugh

- do good deeds for her

- set up date nights

Other

- go to church

- try to live the seven laws of success: law of pure potentiality, law of giving, law of karma, law of least effort, law of intention and desire, law of detachment, law of darma (purpose)

Jessica's List of Platinum Practices™

- In the morning, do yoga stretches and take vitamins, fish oil and probiotic

- Go to Mass and say the Rosary, daily if possible

- Workout, do sit-ups, walk, and get lymphatic massage

- Recognize my own needs and speak up for them

- Eat my main meal early in the day and juice daily

- Oversee travel arrangements myself

- Regularly file papers, and clean out my drawers and closets

- Do pelvic floor stretches and wear nightguard to bed

Jessica keeps her list of practices next to the calendar in her kitchen, and also keeps a copy next to her computer and in her purse. She refers to them daily and knows the more she mindfully monitors them and practices them, the better she feels, the more productive she is, and the more she is control of her time and her energy.

Conclusion

You are living and working in one of the most challenging, demanding and complex times in human history. However, this does not mean you have to fall into the negative spin factor trap caused by multitasking, modern technology and unrealistic expectations about how you "should" live your life and do your work.

You can make a conscious choice to live and work in the new way—a way that is inspired by Eastern practices and shows how you can achieve better results and perform at your optimum level by:

- Rebooting your internal computer daily

- Feeding your body to boost your brainpower and fuel your business

- Putting yourself first in your calendar and managing your time in a strategic, focused way

- Getting organized and clearing away the clutter to de-stress and release your creative potential

- Breathing more deeply and fully

- Cultivating more *Yin* for balance and enhanced productivity and enjoyment of life, and

- Mindfully monitoring what matters most to stay on track and realize your vision for the impact you want to have on the world.

To access additional resources to support your transition to this new way of living and working, visit ErinOwen.com/BookResources.

Ultimately, by experimenting with the Eastern-inspired performance secrets I have shared with you, you will refuel, recharge and re-energize yourself, enabling you to take back control of your time and your energy.

The Bottom Line

Say "YES!" to activating your highest potential so you can make your mark on the world and catapult yourself to a higher level of living and working that positively changes the world.

Thank you!

Erin

Take it to the Next Level

If you want to take these ideas further to more deeply transform your life and your potential, read on to learn what might work best for you, your team, your organization.

Stay in Touch, Stay Inspired, Stay Motivated

In my blog posts and emails, I write about the challenges of daily life and what we can do about it, share success stories to inspire you, and also make announcements about upcoming events and retreats. The best way to stay connected with this philosophy of living and working in a smarter way is to sign-up for my mailing list. You can do this at ErinOwen.com.

Go Deeper and Learn More

My foundational course titled *Boost Your Performance In and Out* of the Office, teaches you how to reduce the complexity in your life and increase your energy, effectiveness and impact. It features 6 core lessons, each with 3 targeted tips, for a total of 18 ideas to simplify and transform your life. Included are a fully detailed, 61-page workbook, an easy-to-follow quick guide, and professionally recorded audio lessons.

You can take the course on your own at your own pace, either by reading the lessons or listening to them via audio recordings. You can also choose to add-on six 20-minute coaching sessions (one after each lesson) for additional support. Learn more at ErinOwen.com/Author.

Speaking and Training Services

I offer a variety of keynotes and training programs that share the core principles and strategies from the 6 pillars of my one-of-a-kind Transformational System:

1. Vision & Mindset

2. Time Management & Personal Organization

3. Health & Well-being

4. Relationships, Communication & Personal Fulfillment

5. Career & Finances

6. Creativity & Spirituality

With my interactive, dynamic presentation and teaching style, I empower and educate my audience to:

- Shift from "overwhelmed" to a new, energized way of living and working.

- Powerfully harmonize work and life to move beyond "just balance."

- Create meaningful connections with key people at work and home to develop creativity and reignite passion.

- Revolutionize work performance so "time off" is once again carefree and deeply rejuvenating.

Learn more at ErinOwen.com/Speaking.

Private Coaching Support

As a coach, I partner with my clients. Through private coaching sessions and powerful retreat days, the focus is to clarify your life vision, create manageable goals to bridge the gap between your current challenges and what you want in your life, and make tangible progress to transform your life to be more meaningful and abundant. To learn more, visit ErinOwen.com/Private-Coaching-Leaders/.

Let's Talk

To schedule a 15-minute call with me, or invest your time in a 90-minute in-depth assessment and coaching session, email me Connect@ErinOwen.com or learn more at ErinOwen.com/Appointments/.

Don't Go it Alone!

Whichever next step you take, be aware that swimming upstream in a culture that challenges your every move can be tough. Make sure you surround yourself with a supportive, encouraging team.

Here's to you taking back control of your time and energy, so you can experience more meaning and joy in your life!

Erin